D1512553

POPE FRANCIS

LIFE AFTER
THE PANDEMIC

Preface by
Cardinal MICHAEL CZERNY, SJ

LIBRERIA
EDITRICE
VATICANA

© Copyright 2020 – Libreria Editrice Vaticana
00120 Città del Vaticano
Tel. 06.698.45780 - Fax 06.698.84716
E-mail: commerciale.lev@spc.va

Printed Edition
ISBN 978-88-266-0446-6

Digital Edition
ISBN 978-88-266-0433-6

www.vatican.va
www.libreriaeditricevaticana.va

PREFACE

by Cardinal MICHAEL CZERNY, SJ

In the early months of 2020, Pope Francis frequently reflected on the coronavirus pandemic as it took hold of the human family. Collected here are eight significant spoken and written texts dated from 27 March to 22 April. To whom did he speak, and how? What did he say, and why?

Beyond their specific occasions, these eight texts could be read together as a single development of his thought and as a rich message to humanity. This collection has two objectives. The first is to suggest direction, keys, and guidelines for rebuilding a better world that might be born from this crisis of humanity. The second objective is, in the midst of so much suffering and bewilderment, to sow hope. The Pope clearly bases this hope on faith, "because with God life never dies".[1]

We begin with the *Urbi et orbi* messages, the title of a major papal address of long

---

[1] Urbi et orbi *Address during the Extraordinary Moment of Prayer "Why Are You Afraid?"*, Sagrato of Saint Peter's Basilica, 27 March 2020.

tradition. Twice in 17 days, Pope Francis solemnly addressed and blessed the city (*Urbi*) of Rome, of which he is Bishop, and the entire world (*orbi*): on 27 March, an occasion without precedent, at the extraordinary prayer of adoration in St Peter's Square; and on 12 April, as traditionally on Easter Sunday.

The *Urbi et orbi* invites all humanity to listen just as inclusively as did *Laudato si'* in 2015 – "I wish to address every person living on this planet"[2] – and *Querida Amazonia* in February 2020 which spoke "to the People of God and to all persons of good will".

Though applying strictly only to two, the *Urbi et orbi*, in some way, characterizes all eight texts in this collection about the COVID-19 crisis. They speak to the needs and suffering of people in various local situations in the Pope's very personal, heartfelt, committed and hopeful manner. They are also truly universal, not only because the virus menaces everyone without discrimination, but especially because the post-COVID-19 world must be for everyone to shape. These eight texts show Pope Francis's warm and inclusive approach. It does not reduce people to bits to be counted, measured and managed,

---

[2] Encyclical Letter *Laudato si'*, 25 May 2015, 3.

but binds everyone together in humanity and spirit. And then with no less warmth and inclusivity, the Pope challenges everyone – no matter how high or humble – to dare to do good, to do better. We can! We must!

"From this colonnade that embraces Rome and the whole world, may God's blessing come down upon you as a consoling embrace".[3] The *Urbi et orbi* invites heads of state and government, the world's decision-makers, "those in positions of leadership",[4] the privileged who belong to "a small part of the human family [that] has moved ahead, while the majority has remained behind".[5] The Holy Father questions and challenges "all who have responsibility in conflicts"[6] and occupy a place at "the table of economic power".[7]

"I encourage political leaders to work actively for the common good",[8] Francis de-

---

[3] *Why Are You Afraid?*, op. cit.

[4] *Wednesday Audience Catechesis on the occasion of the 50th Earth Day, "Overcoming Global Challenges"*, 22 April 2020.

[5] *Homily, "Egoism: An Even Worse Virus", Second Sunday of Easter*, 19 April 2020.

[6] Urbi et orbi *Address, "Like a new flame", Sunday of Easter*, 12 April 2020.

[7] *Easter Letter to Popular Movements, "To an invisible army"*, 12 April 2020.

[8] *Like a New Flame*, op. cit.

clares, and many countries have in fact shared information, knowledge and resources. At the same time, the Pope's gratitude and affection go to "all who work diligently to guarantee the essential services necessary for civil society, and to the law enforcement and military personnel who in many countries have helped ease people's difficulties and sufferings".[9]

In this unique collection, Pope Francis also hears and sees many who are usually kept silent and invisible. On Easter he wrote to the grassroots movements or organizations of the informal or popular economy. "Our civilization … needs to downshift, take stock, and renew itself. You are the indispensable builders of this change that can no longer be put off".[10] And in a brief message, "I now want to greet the world of street newspapers and especially their vendors, who are mostly homeless, severely marginalized, unemployed".[11] This is probably the first time such people have ever been taken into account, much less greeted respectfully, and he continues: "In these days, looking at the poorest can help us all become

---

[9] *Ibid.*
[10] *To an Invisible Army, op. cit.*
[11] *Letter to the World of Street Newspapers,* 21 April 2020.

aware of what's really happening to us and of our true condition".[12]

Addressing each and everyone directly, not from on high or in the abstract, Pope Francis reaches out with fatherly affection and compassion to make his own the suffering and sacrifice of so very many people: "May the Lord of life welcome the departed into His kingdom and grant comfort and hope to those still suffering, especially the elderly and those who are alone. May He never withdraw His consolation and help from those who are especially vulnerable, such as persons who work in nursing homes, or live in barracks and prisons".[13] And the family album goes on: "doctors, nurses, supermarket employees, cleaners, caregivers, providers of transport, law and order forces, volunteers, priests, religious men and women"[14] and "fathers, mothers, grandparents and teachers … showing our children, in small everyday gestures, how to face up to and navigate a crisis by adjusting their routines, lifting their gaze and fostering prayer".[15] He sympathizes:

---

[12] *Ibid.*
[13] *Like a New Flame, op. cit.*
[14] *Why Are You Afraid?, op. cit.*
[15] *Ibid.*

"How difficult it is to stay at home for those who live in tiny, ramshackle dwellings, or for the homeless! How difficult it is for migrants, those who are deprived of freedom, and those in rehabilitation from an addiction".[16] And "I think of all the people, especially women, who multiply loaves of bread in soup kitchens: two onions and a package of rice make up a delicious stew for hundreds of children. I think of the sick, I think of the elderly [and of] small farmers and their families who work hard to produce healthy food without destroying nature, without hoarding, without exploiting people's needs".[17]

So what does the Pope say, and why? At the highest level, one "alternative is the self-ishness of particular interests and the temptation of a return to the past, at the risk of severely damaging the peaceful coexistence and development of future generations";[18] and with this comes the "danger that we will forget those who are left behind. The risk is that we may then be struck by an even worse virus, that of *selfish indifference*".[19]

---

[16] *To an Invisible Army, op. cit.*
[17] *Ibid.*
[18] *Like a New Flame, op. cit.*
[19] *Egoism: An Even Worse Virus, op. cit.*

Let us "be profoundly shaken by what is happening all around us"[20] and recognize ourselves "as part of a single family and support one another".[21] "The time has come to eliminate inequalities, to heal the injustice that is undermining the health of the entire human family!".[22]

The time has arrived to prepare for fundamental change in a post-COVID. In a handwritten note to an Argentinean judge, the Pope emphasizes: "it is important to prepare ourselves for what follows".[23] And in a recent interview not contained in this collection, recording his responses to the questions of a British journalist, he states that the "aftermath has already begun to be revealed as tragic and painful, which is why we must be thinking about it now".[24]

As members of one human family and residents of our only common home, a dangerous selfishness infects many more of us

---

[20] *Ibid.*

[21] *Like a New Flame, op. cit.*

[22] *Egoism: An Even Worse Virus, op. cit.*

[23] *Letter to Dr. Roberto Andrés Gallardo. "Preparing for Afterwards Is Important"*, 30 March 2020.

[24] AUSTEN IVEREIGH, *"A Time of Great Uncertainty"*, *An Interview with Pope Francis*, 8 April 2020.

than COVID-19. "[We] have failed in our responsibility to be guardians and stewards of the earth. *We need only take a frank look at the facts to see that our common home is falling into serious disrepair.* We have polluted it, we have despoiled it, endangering our very lives... We have no future if we destroy the very environment that sustains us".[25] Now, facing the pandemic, we have widely and vividly experienced our inter-connectedness in vulnerability. Much of humanity has responded to that vulnerability with resolve and solidarity. We have proven that we can do it, we can change, and it is now for us to translate those traits into a permanent conversion of resolve and solidarity to cope with the larger and longer-term threats.

The time has also come to reflect on economic activities and work. Just going back to what was being done before the pandemic may seem the obvious, practical choice, but why not switch to something better? Why reinvest in fossil fuels, monoculture farming and rainforest destruction when we know they worsen our environmental crisis? Why resume the arms industry with its terrible

---

[25] *Overcoming Global Challenges, op. cit.*

waste of resources and useless destruction? The Pope is "worried by the hypocrisy of certain political personalities who speak of facing up to the crisis ... but who in the meantime manufacture weapons".[26] Surely, we need "arms" of a different sort to fight disease and ease suffering, starting with all the equipment needed for clinics and hospitals worldwide. Let us courageously think outside the box. After what we have already been through this year, we should not be afraid to venture out on new paths and propose innovative solutions.

The work of care certainly requires recognition, support and innovation. The pandemic has shown how fundamental and strategic care is. However, in many countries it is an ignored sector: wages are low, hospitals are understaffed, shifts are heavy, proper contracts and benefits are missing. Many caregivers are informal: "working on your own or in the grassroots economy, you have no steady income to get you through this hard time".[27] Many are immigrants. Why do employees in other sectors that make a much less important contribution earn vastly more than care work-

---

[26] IVEREIGH, *A Time of Great Uncertainty*, op. cit.
[27] *To an Invisible Army*, op. cit.

ers? Moreover, valuing care work would significantly improve the situation of women, since they are numerically predominant in this sector – all the more reason why care work should not be marginal. Let's show the same operational agility demonstrated in successfully locking down the virus in rehabilitating and enhancing the entire care industry.

This logic should extend to the whole informal sector. "Many of you live from day to day, without any type of legal guarantee to protect you".[28] These are the workers with the least protection during the lockdown, even though many are just as essential as those with steady jobs. "Street vendors, recyclers, carnies, small farmers, construction workers, dressmakers, the different kinds of caregivers: ... and the lockdowns are becoming unbearable".[29] The Pope asks us to show courage in innovation, trying out new solutions and setting out on new paths.

Looking ahead, let us read the signs that COVID-19 has brightly displayed. Let us not forget how loss of human contact during this time profoundly impoverished us when separated from neighbors, friends, co-work-

---

[28] *Ibid.*
[29] *Ibid.*

ers, and especially family, including the utter cruelty of being unable to accompany the dying in their last moments and then mourn them properly. Let us not take togetherness for granted in the future but rediscover it and find ways to strengthen it.

Challenging and changing current industries, recognizing non-formal work and fortifying the work of care are now on the public agenda. "My hope is that governments understand that technocratic paradigms (whether state-centered or market-driven) are not enough to address this crisis or the other great problems affecting humankind. Now more than ever, persons, communities and peoples must be put at the center, united to heal, to care and to share".[30]

By now we understand that *everyone* is involved and implicated because of COVID-19: inequality, climate change and poor governance threaten everyone. We should also understand that changes must be made to the paradigms and systems that put the whole world in jeopardy. Our life after the pandemic must not be a replica of what went before, no matter who used to benefit dispro-

---

[30] *Ibid.*

portionately. "Let us show mercy to those who are most vulnerable; for only in this way will we build a new world".[31]

COVID-19 has allowed us to put self-ishness and competition to the test, and the answer is: if we continue to accept and even demand ruthless competition among individual, corporate and national interests where the losers are destroyed, then the winners will ultimately lose along with the rest because this pattern is unsustainable at every scale, from the microscopic virus to ocean currents and worldwide atmosphere and supplies of fresh water. A new era of solidarity would have all humans on the same plane of dignity, each taking responsibility and contributing so that all, oneself and others and future generations, may flourish.

Together with vision, commitment and action, Pope Francis has demonstrated how prayer is fundamental for redirecting our gaze in hope, especially when hope becomes tenuous and struggles to survive. "How many are praying, offering and interceding for the good of all. Prayer and quiet service: these are our victorious weapons".[32] While leading the

---

[31] *Egoism: An even worse virus, op. cit.*
[32] *Why Are You Afraid?, op. cit.*

world in adoration on 27 March, the Holy Father taught that to pray means:

- to listen, to let ourselves be troubled by what we are living, to face the wind and the silence, the darkness and the rain, to let the ambulance sirens disturb us;
- to recognize that we are not self-sufficient and therefore to entrust ourselves to God;
- to contemplate the Lord's body in order to be permeated by His way of doing, to dialogue with Him in order to welcome, accompany, support as He did;
- to learn from Jesus to take up the cross and together with Him to take on the suffering of many;
- to imitate Him in our frailty so that, via our weakness, salvation enters the world; and
- to look to Mary, *Health of the People and Star of the stormy Sea* and ask her to teach us to say "Yes" every day and be available, concretely and generously.

Prayer becomes the way to discover how to become disciples and missionaries today, embodying unconditional love in widely varied circumstances for every human being and every creature. This path can lead us towards a different outlook on the world, its contradictions and its possibilities, it can teach us day after day how to convert our relationships, our lifestyles, our expectations and our policies towards integral human development and the fullness of life. Therefore, listening, contemplation, prayer are an integral part of the struggle against inequalities and exclusions and for life-sustaining alternatives.

Pope Francis says to every reader of this collection, every community and society, *Urbi et orbi*: "I pray for you, I pray with you. I want to ask God our Father to bless you, to fill you with His love, and to defend you on this path, giving you the strength that keeps us standing tall and that never disappoints: hope".[33]

---

[33] *To an Invisible Army, op. cit.*

POPE FRANCIS

LIFE AFTER
THE PANDEMIC

WHY ARE YOU AFRAID?

"When[34] evening had come" (*Mk* 4:35). The Gospel passage we have just heard begins like this. For weeks now, it has been evening. Thick darkness has gathered over our squares, our streets and our cities; it has taken over our lives, filling everything with a deafening silence and a distressing void, that stops everything as it passes by; we feel it in the air, we notice in people's gestures, their glances give them away. We find ourselves afraid and lost. Like the disciples in the Gospel we were caught off guard by an unexpected, turbulent storm. We have realized that we are on the same boat, all of us fragile and disoriented, but at the same time important and needed, all of us called to row together, each of us in need of comforting the other. On this boat… are all of us. Just like those disciples, who spoke anxiously with one voice, saying "We are perishing" (v. 38), so we too have realized that we cannot go on thinking of ourselves, but only together can we do this.

---

[34] Urbi et orbi *Address during the Extraordinary Moment of Prayer*, Sagrato of St Peter's Basilica, 27 March 2020.

It is easy to recognize ourselves in this story. What is harder to understand is Jesus's attitude. While His disciples are quite naturally alarmed and desperate, He is in the stern, in the part of the boat that sinks first. And what does He do? In spite of the tempest, He sleeps on soundly, trusting in the Father; this is the only time in the Gospels we see Jesus sleeping. When He wakes up, after calming the wind and the waters, He turns to the disciples in a reproaching voice: "Why are you afraid? Have you no faith?" (v. 40).

Let us try to understand. In what does the lack of the disciples' faith consist, as contrasted with Jesus's trust? They had not stopped believing in Him; in fact, they called on Him. But we see how they call on Him: "Teacher, do you not care if we perish?" (v. 38). *You do not care*: they think that Jesus is not interested in them, does not care about them. One of the things that hurts us and our families most when we hear it said is: "Do you not care about me?" It is a phrase that wounds and unleashes storms in our hearts. It would have shaken Jesus too. Because He, more than anyone, cares about us. Indeed, once they have called on Him, He saves His disciples from their discouragement.

The storm exposes our vulnerability and uncovers those false and superfluous certainties around which we have constructed our daily schedules, our projects, our habits and priorities. It shows us how we have allowed to become dull and feeble the very things that nourish, sustain and strengthen our lives and our communities. The tempest lays bare all our prepackaged ideas and forgetfulness of what nourishes our people's souls; all those attempts that anesthetize us with ways of thinking and acting that supposedly "save" us, but instead prove incapable of putting us in touch with our roots and keeping alive the memory of those who have gone before us. We deprive ourselves of the antibodies we need to confront adversity.

In this storm, the façade of those stereotypes with which we camouflaged our egos, always worrying about our image, has fallen away, uncovering once more that (blessed) common belonging, of which we cannot be deprived: our belonging as brothers and sisters.

"Why are you afraid? Have you no faith?". Lord, your word this evening strikes us and regards us, all of us. In this world, that you love more than we do, we have gone ahead at breakneck speed, feeling powerful and able to do anything. Greedy for profit, we let ourselves get caught up in things, and lured away by haste. We did not stop at your re-

proach to us, we were not shaken awake by wars or injustice across the world, nor did we listen to the cry of the poor or of our ailing planet. We carried on regardless, thinking we would stay healthy in a world that was sick. Now that we are in a stormy sea, we implore you: "Wake up, Lord!".

"Why are you afraid? Have you no faith?". Lord, you are calling to us, calling us to faith which is not so much believing that you exist, but coming to you and trusting in you. This Lent your call reverberates urgently: "Be converted!", "Return to me with all your heart" (*Joel* 2:12). You are calling on us to seize this time of trial as a *time of choosing*. It is not the time of your judgement, but of our judgement: a time to choose what matters and what passes away, a time to separate what is necessary from what is not. It is a time to get our lives back on track with regard to you, Lord, and to others. We can look to so many exemplary companions for the journey, who, even though fearful, have reacted by giving their lives. This is the force of the Spirit poured out and fashioned in courageous and generous self-denial. It is the life in the Spirit that can redeem, value and demonstrate how our lives are woven together and sustained by ordinary people – often forgotten people – who

do not appear in newspaper and magazine headlines nor on the grand catwalks of the latest show, but who without any doubt are in these very days writing the decisive events of our time: doctors, nurses, supermarket employees, cleaners, caregivers, providers of transport, law and order forces, volunteers, priests, religious men and women and so very many others who have understood that no one reaches salvation by themselves. In the face of so much suffering, where the authentic development of our peoples is assessed, we experience the priestly prayer of Jesus: "That they may all be one" (*Jn* 17:21). How many people every day are exercising patience and offering hope, taking care to sow not panic but a shared responsibility. How many fathers, mothers, grandparents and teachers are showing our children, in small everyday gestures, how to face up to and navigate a crisis by adjusting their routines, lifting their gaze and fostering prayer. How many are praying, offering and interceding for the good of all. Prayer and quiet service: these are our victorious weapons.

"Why are you afraid? Have you no faith?". Faith begins when we realize we are in need of salvation. We are not self-sufficient; by ourselves we flounder: we need the Lord,

like ancient navigators needed the stars. Let us invite Jesus into the boats of our lives. Let us hand over our fears to Him so that He can conquer them. Like the disciples, we will experience that with Him on board there will be no shipwreck. Because this is God's strength: turning to the good everything that happens to us, even the bad things. He brings serenity into our storms, because with God life never dies.

The Lord asks us and, in the midst of our tempest, invites us to reawaken and put into practice that solidarity and hope capable of giving strength, support and meaning to these hours when everything seems to be floundering. The Lord awakens so as to reawaken and revive our Easter faith. We have an anchor: by His cross we have been saved. We have a rudder: by His cross we have been redeemed. We have a hope: by His cross we have been healed and embraced so that nothing and no one can separate us from His redeeming love. In the midst of isolation when we are suffering from a lack of tenderness and chances to meet up, and we experience the loss of so many things, let us once again listen to the proclamation that saves us: He is risen and is living by our side. The Lord asks us from His cross to rediscover the life that awaits us, to look towards those who look to us, to strengthen, recognize and foster the grace that lives within us. Let us not quench the wavering flame (cf. *Is* 42:3) that never falters, and let us allow hope to be rekindled.

Embracing His cross means finding the courage to embrace all the hardships of the present time, abandoning for a moment our eagerness for power and possessions in order to make room for the creativity that only the Spirit is capable of inspiring. It means finding the courage to create spaces where everyone can recognize that they are called, and to allow new forms of hospitality, fraternity and solidarity. By His cross we have been saved in order to embrace hope and let it strengthen and sustain all measures and all possible avenues for helping us protect ourselves and others. Embracing the Lord in order to embrace hope: that is the strength of faith, which frees us from fear and gives us hope.

"Why are you afraid? Have you no faith?". Dear brothers and sisters, from this place that tells of Peter's rock-solid faith, I would like this evening to entrust all of you to the Lord, through the intercession of Mary, Health of the People and Star of the stormy Sea. From this colonnade that embraces Rome and the whole world, may God's blessing come down upon you as a consoling embrace. Lord, may

you bless the world, give health to our bodies and comfort our hearts. You ask us not to be afraid. Yet our faith is weak and we are fearful. But you, Lord, will not leave us at the mercy of the storm. Tell us again: "Do not be afraid" (*Mt* 28:5). And we, together with Peter, "cast all our anxieties onto you, for you care about us" (cf. *1 Pt* 5:7).

Preparing for Afterwards
Is Important

Dear[35] Brother,

Thank you for your message. We are all concerned about the global progression of the pandemic. However, I am edified by the reaction of so many people including doctors, nurses, volunteers, religious and priests, who are risking their lives to attend to the sick and prevent those who are healthy from becoming infected. Some governments have taken exemplary measures with clear priorities to defend the people in their respective countries. It is true that these measures are burdensome for those who find themselves obliged to observe them, but it is always for the common good and, on the whole, the majority of people accept them and approach them with a positive attitude.

Governments who approach the crisis in this way demonstrate the priority of their decision making: people first. This is important, because we all realize that defending the peo-

---

[35] *Letter to Roberto Andrés Gallardo*, 30 March 2020.

ple of a country in the current situation entails economic hardship. However, it would be sad to opt for the contrary, which would lead to the death of many people, in one sense a kind of viral genocide.

On Friday we had a meeting with the Dicastery for Promoting Integral Human Development to reflect on the present time and the future. It is important to prepare ourselves for what follows. We can already see some consequences that need to be faced: hunger, especially for people without permanent employment (casual workers, etc.), violence, the appearance of loan sharks (who may become the real plague of our society in the near future, inhuman criminals), etc.

There is an interesting vision of a possible future economic landscape by the economist Mariana Mazzucato, professor at University College London (*The Value of Everything. Making and Taking in the Global Economy*, Penguin 2019). I think it helps to think about the future.

Warmest greetings to your mother, please don't forget to pray for me as I do for you. May the Lord bless you and the Blessed Virgin protect you.

Fraternally

LIKE A NEW FLAME

Dear[36] Brothers and Sisters, Happy Easter!

Today the Church's proclamation echoes throughout the world: "Jesus Christ is risen!" – "He is truly risen!".

Like a new flame this Good News springs up in the night: the night of a world already faced with epochal challenges and now oppressed by a pandemic severely testing our whole human family. In this night, the Church's voice rings out: "Christ, my hope, has arisen!" (*Easter Sequence*).

This is a different "contagion", a message transmitted from heart to heart – for every human heart awaits this Good News. It is the contagion of hope: "Christ, my hope, is risen!". This is no magic formula that makes problems vanish. No, the resurrection of Christ is not that. Instead, it is the victory of love over the root of evil, a victory that does not "by-pass" suffering and death, but passes through them, opening a path in the abyss, transforming evil into good: this is the unique hallmark of the power of God.

---

[36] Urbi et orbi *Address*, *Sunday of Easter*, Saint Peter's Basilica, 12 April 2020.

The Risen Lord is also the Crucified One, not someone else. In His glorious body he bears indelible wounds: wounds that have become windows of hope. Let us turn our gaze to Him that He may heal the wounds of an afflicted humanity.

Today my thoughts turn in the first place to the many who have been directly affected by the coronavirus: the sick, those who have died and family members who mourn the loss of their loved ones, to whom, in some cases, they were unable even to bid a final farewell. May the Lord of life welcome the departed into His kingdom and grant comfort and hope to those still suffering, especially the elderly and those who are alone. May He never withdraw His consolation and help from those who are especially vulnerable, such as persons who work in nursing homes, or live in barracks and prisons. For many, this is an Easter of solitude lived amid the sorrow and hardship that the pandemic is causing, from physical suffering to economic difficulties.

This disease has not only deprived us of human closeness, but also of the possibility of receiving in person the consolation that flows from the sacraments, particularly the Eucharist and Reconciliation. In many countries, it has not been possible to approach them, but the Lord has not left us alone! United in our prayer, we are convinced that He has laid His hand upon us (cf. *Ps* 138:5), firmly reassuring us: Do not be afraid, "I have risen and I am with you still!" (cf. *Roman Missal*, Entrance Antiphon, Mass of Easter Sunday).

May Jesus, our Passover, grant strength and hope to doctors and nurses, who everywhere offer a witness of care and love for our neighbors, to the point of exhaustion and not infrequently at the expense of their own health. Our gratitude and affection go to them, to all who work diligently to guarantee the essential services necessary for civil society, and to the law enforcement and military personnel who in many countries have helped ease people's difficulties and sufferings.

In these weeks, the lives of millions of people have suddenly changed. For many, remaining at home has been an opportunity to reflect, to withdraw from the frenetic pace of life, stay with loved ones and enjoy their company. For many, though, this is also a time of worry about an uncertain future, about jobs that are at risk and about other consequences of the current crisis. I encourage political leaders to work actively for the common good, to provide the means and resources needed to enable everyone to lead a dignified life and, when circumstances allow, to assist them in resuming their normal daily activities.

This is not a time for indifference, because the whole world is suffering and needs to be united in facing the pandemic. May the risen Jesus grant hope to all the poor, to those living on the peripheries, to refugees and the homeless. May these, the most vulnerable of our brothers and sisters living in the cities and peripheries of every part of the world, not be abandoned. Let us ensure that they do not lack basic necessities (all the more difficult to find now that many businesses are closed) such as medicine and especially the possibility of adequate health care. In light of the present circumstances, may international sanctions be relaxed, since these make it difficult for countries on which they have been imposed to provide adequate support to their citizens, and may all nations be put in a position to meet the greatest needs of the moment through the reduction, if not the forgiveness, of the debt burdening the balance sheets of the poorest nations.

This is not a time for self-centeredness, because the challenge we are facing is shared by all, without distinguishing between persons. Among the many areas of the world affected by the coronavirus, I think in a special way of Europe. After the Second World War, this continent was able to rise again, thanks to a concrete spirit of solidarity that enabled it to overcome the rivalries of the past. It is more urgent than ever, especially in the present circumstances, that these rivalries do not regain force, but that all recognize themselves as part of a single family and support one another. The European Union is presently facing an epochal challenge, on which will depend not only its future but that of the whole world. Let us not lose the opportunity to give further proof of solidarity, also by turning to innovative solutions. The only alternative is the selfishness of particular interests and the temptation of a return to the past, at the risk of severely damaging the peaceful coexistence and development of future generations.

This is not a time for division. May Christ our peace enlighten all who have responsibility in conflicts, that they may have the courage to support the appeal for an immediate global ceasefire in all corners of the world. This is not a time for continuing to manufacture and deal in arms, spending vast amounts of money that ought to be used to care for others and save lives. Rather, may this be a time for finally ending the long war that has caused such great bloodshed in beloved Syria, the conflict in Yemen and the hostilities in Iraq and in Lebanon. May this be the time when Israelis and Palestinians resume dialogue in order to find a stable and lasting solution that will allow both to live in peace. May the sufferings of the people who live in the eastern regions of Ukraine come to an end. May the terrorist attacks carried out against so many innocent people in different African countries come to an end.

This is not a time for forgetfulness. The crisis we are facing should not make us forget the many other crises that bring suffering to so many people. May the Lord of life be close to all those in Asia and Africa who are experiencing grave humanitarian crises, as in the Province of Cabo Delgado in the north of Mozambique. May He warm the hearts of the many refugees displaced because of wars, drought and famine. May He grant protection to migrants and refugees, many of them children, who are living in unbearable conditions, especially in Libya and on the border between Greece and Turkey. And I do not want to forget the island of Lesbos. In Venezuela, may He enable concrete and immediate solutions to be reached that can permit international assistance to a population suffering from the grave political, socio-economic and health situation.

Dear brothers and sisters,

Indifference, self-centeredness, division and forgetfulness are not words we want to hear at this time. We want to ban these words for ever! They seem to prevail when fear and death overwhelm us, that is, when we do not let the Lord Jesus triumph in our hearts and lives. May Christ, who has already defeated death and opened for us the way to eternal salvation, dispel the darkness of our suffering humanity and lead us into the light of his glorious day, a day that knows no end.

With these thoughts, I would like to wish all of you a happy Easter.

To an Invisible Army

Dear[37] Friends,

I often recall our previous meetings: two at the Vatican and one in Santa Cruz de la Sierra, and I must tell you that this "souvenir" warms my heart. It brings me closer to you, and helps me re-live so many dialogues we had during those times. I think of all the beautiful projects that emerged from those conversations and took shape and have become reality. Now, in the midst of this pandemic, I think of you in a special way and wish to express my closeness to you.

In these days of great anxiety and hardship, many have used war-like metaphors to refer to the pandemic we are experiencing. If the struggle against COVID-19 is a war, then you are truly an invisible army, fighting in the most dangerous trenches; an army whose only weapons are solidarity, hope, and community spirit, all revitalizing at a time when no one can save themselves alone. As I told you in our meetings, to me you are social poets because, from the forgotten peripheries where

---

[37] *Letter to Popular Movements*, 12 April 2020.

you live, you create admirable solutions for the most pressing problems afflicting the marginalized.

I know that you nearly never receive the recognition that you deserve, because you are truly invisible to the system. Market solutions do not reach the peripheries, and State protection is hardly visible there. Nor do you have the resources to substitute for its functioning. You are looked upon with suspicion when through community organization you try to move beyond philanthropy or when, instead of resigning and hoping to catch some crumbs that fall from the table of economic power, you claim your rights. You often feel rage and powerlessness at the sight of persistent inequalities and when any excuse at all is sufficient for maintaining those privileges. Nevertheless, you do not resign yourselves to complaining: you roll up your sleeves and keep working for your families, your communities, and the common good. Your resilience helps me, challenges me, and teaches me a great deal.

I think of all the people, especially women, who multiply loaves of bread in soup kitchens: two onions and a package of rice make up a delicious stew for hundreds of children. I think of the sick, I think of the elderly. They never appear in the news, nor do small farmers and their families who work hard to produce healthy food without destroying nature, without hoarding, without exploiting people's needs. I want you to know that our Heavenly Father watches over you, values you, appreciates you, and supports you in your commitment.

How difficult it is to stay at home for those who live in tiny, ramshackle dwellings, or for the homeless! How difficult it is for migrants, those who are deprived of freedom, and those in rehabilitation from an addiction. You are there shoulder to shoulder with them, helping them to make things less difficult, less painful. I congratulate and thank you with all my heart.

My hope is that governments understand that technocratic paradigms (whether state-centered or market-driven) are not enough to address this crisis or the other great problems affecting humankind. Now more than ever, persons, communities and peoples must be put at the center, united to heal, to care and to share.

I know that you have been excluded from the benefits of globalization. You do not enjoy the superficial pleasures that anesthetize so many consciences, yet you always suffer from the harm they produce. The ills that afflict everyone hit you twice as hard. Many of you live from day to day, without any type of legal guarantee to protect you. Street vendors, recyclers, carnies, small farmers, construction workers, dressmakers, the different kinds of caregivers: you who are informal, working on your own or in the grassroots economy, you have no steady income to get you through this hard time ... and the lockdowns are becoming unbearable. This may be the time to consider a universal basic wage which would acknowledge and dignify the noble, essential tasks you carry out. It would ensure and concretely achieve the ideal, at once so human and so Christian, of no worker without rights.

Moreover, I urge you to reflect on "life after the pandemic," for while this storm shall pass, its grave consequences are already being felt. You are not helpless. You have the culture, the method, and most of all, the wisdom that are kneaded with the leaven of feeling the suffering of others as your own. I want all of us to think about the project of integral human development that we long for and that is based on the central role and initiative of the people in all their diversity, as well as on universal access to those three *Ts* that you defend: *Trabajo* (*work*), *Techo* (*housing*) and *Tierra* (*land* and food).

I hope that this time of danger will free us from operating on automatic pilot, shake our sleepy consciences and allow a humanist and ecological conversion that puts an end to the idolatry of money and places human life and dignity at the center. Our civilization – so competitive, so individualistic, with its frenetic rhythms of production and consumption, its extravagant luxuries, its disproportionate profits for just a few – needs to downshift, take stock, and renew itself.

You are the indispensable builders of this change that can no longer be put off. Moreover, when you testify that to change is possible, your voice is authoritative. You have known crises and hardships ... that you manage to transform – with modesty, dignity, commitment, hard work and solidarity – into a promise of life for your families and your communities.

Stand firm in your struggle and care for each other as brothers and sisters. I pray for you, I pray with you. I want to ask God our Father to bless you, to fill you with His love, and to defend you on this path, giving you the strength that keeps us standing tall and that never disappoints: hope. Please pray for me, because I need it too.

Fraternally

A Plan to Rise up Again

"Suddenly[38] Jesus met them and greeted them, saying: 'Rejoice'" (cf. *Mt* 28:9). It is the first word of the Risen One after Mary Magdalene and the other Mary discovered the empty tomb and came across the angel. The Lord meets them to transform their mourning into joy and to comfort them in the midst of affliction (cf. *Jer* 31:13).He is the Risen One who wants to resurrect the women to a new life and, with them, all of humanity. He wants us to begin to participate from now in the resurrected condition that awaits us.

An invitation to joy could seem like a provocation, and even like a bad joke in the face of the serious consequences we are suffering from COVID-19. Like the disciples at Emmaus, some could think of it as a gesture of ignorance or irresponsibility (cf. *Lk* 24:17-19).

Like the first disciples who went to the tomb, we have been living surrounded by an atmosphere of pain and uncertainty that makes us wonder: "Who will roll away the

---

[38] The original text written in Spanish was published by "Vida Nueva" on 17 April 2020. This English translation has been carried out by LEV staff.

stone for us from the entrance to the tomb?" (*Mk* 16:3). How can we deal with this situation that has completely overwhelmed us?

The impact of everything that is happening, the serious consequences that are already being reported, and those things which we have glimpsed, the pain and mourning for our loved ones, all have the capacity to disorient, distress and paralyze us.

It is the heaviness of the tombstone that imposes itself on the future, and that threatens, with its realism, to bury all hope. It is the heaviness of the anguish of vulnerable and elderly people who are going through quarantine in total solitude; it is the heaviness of those families who cannot now put a plate of food on their tables; it is the heaviness of medical personnel and public servants feeling exhausted and overwhelmed... that heaviness that seems to have the last word.

However, it is moving to highlight the attitude of the women of the Gospel.

Faced with doubts, suffering, perplexity in the face of the situation and even with fear of persecution and of everything that could happen to them, they were able to keep going and not be paralyzed by what was happening. Out of love for the Master, and with that typical, irreplaceable and blessed feminine genius, they were able to confront life as it came, cunningly circumventing obstacles in order to be close to their Lord.

Unlike many of the apostles who fled as prisoners of fear and insecurity – who denied the Lord and escaped (cf. *Jn* 18:25-27) – they [the women], without evading reality or ignoring what was happening, without fleeing or escaping…, they knew how to just be and to accompany others.

The first women disciples, in the midst of darkness and grief, loaded their bags with perfumes and set out to anoint the buried Master (cf. *Mk* 16:1). Recently, we too, like them, have been able to see many who have sought to anoint others, through co-responsibility: they have offered care, and have avoided putting the lives of others at risk.

Unlike those who fled with the hope of saving themselves, we witnessed how neighbors and family members set out with effort and sacrifice, to stay in their homes and thus curb the pandemic.

We were able to discover how many people who were already living and suffering the pandemic of exclusion and indifference continued to strive, to accompany each other and to sustain themselves so that this situation is (or was) less painful.

We saw anointing poured forth from doctors, nurses, supermarket shelf stackers, cleaners, carers, people who transport goods, agents of law and order, volunteers, priests, women religious, grandparents and educators and many others, who had the courage to offer everything they had, to bring some care, calm and courage to the situation.

Although the question remained the same: "Who will roll away the stone from the tomb?" (*Mk* 16:3), all of them did not stop giving what they felt they could give, and had to give. It was precisely there, in the midst of their cares and concerns, that the women disciples were surprised by an overwhelming announcement: "He is not here, He is risen".

His anointing was not an anointing for death, but for life. Their watching and accompanying the Lord, even in death and in the midst of great despair, had not been in vain, but had allowed them to be anointed by the Resurrection: they were not alone, He was alive and preceded them on their way.

Only this overwhelming piece of news was able to break the cycle which prevented them from seeing that the stone had already been rolled away; and that the perfume poured forth could diffuse further than the reality which threatened them.

This is the source of our joy and hope, which transforms our actions: our anointings, dedication... our watching and accompanying in all possible ways at this time are not, and will not be, in vain; they are not a dedication to death.

Every time we take part in the Passion of the Lord, we accompany the passion of our brothers and sisters; living that same passion too, our ears will hear the novelty of the Resurrection: we are not alone, the Lord precedes us on our way, removing the stones that block us. This good news made those women retrace their steps to look for the apostles and the disciples who remained hidden, so as to tell them: He "reawakened to that same life (naturally in a new form) which death has destroyed".[39] This is our hope, the hope that cannot be stolen, silenced or contaminated. The whole life of service and love that you have given in this time will pulse again. It is enough to open a crack so that the anointing that the Lord wants to give us expands with an unstoppable force and allows us to contemplate the reality of suffering with a renewing outlook.

[39] ROMANO GUARDINI, *The Lord*, Gateway Editions – Regnery Publications, Washington, DC 1996[2], 473.

And, like the women of the Gospel, we too are invited again and again to retrace our steps and allow ourselves to be transformed by this announcement: the Lord, with his newness, can always renew our life and that of our community.[40] In this wasteland, the Lord is committed to the regeneration of beauty and the rebirth of hope: "Behold, I am doing something new: right now it is sprouting, don't you see it?" (*Is* 43:19). God never abandons His people, He is always close to them, especially when pain becomes more present.

If we have learned anything in all this time, it is that no one saves himself. Borders fall, walls collapse and all fundamentalist discourse dissolves before an almost imperceptible presence that manifests the fragility of which we are made. Easter summons us and invites us to remember His presence, which is discreet and respectful, generous and reconciling, capable of neither breaking the cracked reed nor extinguishing the wick that burns weakly (cf. *Is* 42:2-3); so that the new life that He wants to give us all, might pulsate. It is the breath of the Spirit that opens horizons,

---

[40] Cf. Apostolic Exhortation *Evangelii gaudium*, 24 November 2013, 11.

awakens creativity and renews us in fraternity to say I am *present* (or *here I am*) before the enormous and imperative task that awaits us. It is a matter of urgency to discern and find the pulse of the Spirit to give impetus, together with others, to dynamics that can witness and channel the new life that the Lord wants to generate at this concrete moment in history. This is the favorable time of the Lord, who is asking us not to conform or content ourselves, let alone justify ourselves with substitutive or palliative logic, which prevents us from sustaining the impact and serious consequences of what we are living. This is the right time to find the courage for a new imagination of the possible, with the realism that only the Gospel can offer us. The Spirit, who does not allow Himself to be locked up or manipulated by fleeting or fixed schemes, modalities and structures, invites us to unite to His movement, which can "make all things new" (*Rev* 21:5).

In this time we realized that it is important "to bring the whole human family together to seek a sustainable and integral development".[41] Every individual action is not an

---

[41] *Laudato si'*, 13.

isolated action, for better or for worse. It has consequences for others, because everything is interconnected in our common home; and if it is the health authorities who order confinement in the home, it is the people who make it possible, aware of their co-responsibility to curb the pandemic. "An emergency like that of Covid-19 is overcome with, above all, the antibodies of solidarity".[42] A lesson that will break all the fatalism in which we may have immersed ourselves, and will allow us to feel once again as creators and protagonists of a common history and, thus, to respond together to so many evils that afflict millions of people around the world. We cannot afford to write present and future history by turning our backs on the suffering of so many. It is the Lord who will ask us again: "Where is your brother?" (*Gen* 4:9), and in the way we respond, may the soul of our peoples be revealed to us. This is the reservoir of hope, faith and charity in which we have been born, and which, for so long, we have anesthetized and silenced.

If we act as one people, even in the face of other epidemics that threaten us, we can make

---

[42] PONTIFICAL ACADEMY FOR LIFE, *Global Pandemic and Universal Brotherhood. Note on the Covid-19 Emergency*, 30 March 2020, 5.

a real impact. Will we be able to act respon-
sibly in the face of the hunger that so many
suffer, knowing that there is food for all? Will
we continue to look the other way with a com-
plicit silence in the face of those wars fuelled
by desires for domination and power? Will we
be willing to change those lifestyles that cause
so many to suffer poverty, and promote and
find the courage to lead a more austere and
human life for a fair sharing of resources? Will
we, as an international community, take the
necessary measures to curb the devastation of
the environment or will we continue to ignore
the evidence? The globalization of indifference
will continue to threaten and tempt us in our
journey... May we find within us the necessary
antibodies of justice, charity and solidarity.
We must not be afraid to live the alternative
– the civilization of love. This is "a civilization
of hope: against anguish and fear, sadness and
discouragement, passivity and tiredness. The
civilization of love is built daily, uninterrupt-
edly. It requires a committed effort by all. For
this reason it requires a committed community
of brothers and sisters".[43]

In this time of tribulation and mourning,
I hope that, where you are, you will be able

---

[43] EDUARDO PIRONIO, *Diálogo con laicos*, Patria
Grande, Buenos Aires 1986.

to experience Jesus, who comes to meet you, greets you and says: "Rejoice" (cf. *Mt* 28:9). And may this greeting mobilize us to invoke and amplify the Good News of the Kingdom of God.

EGOISM: AN EVEN WORSE VIRUS

[…] Dear[44] Brothers and Sisters, in the time of trial that we are presently undergoing, we too, like Thomas, with our fears and our doubts, have experienced our frailty. We need the Lord, who sees beyond that frailty an irrepressible beauty. With Him we rediscover how precious we are even in our vulnerability. We discover that we are like beautiful crystals, fragile and at the same time precious. And if, like crystal, we are transparent before Him, His light – the light of mercy – will shine in us and through us in the world. As the *First Letter of Peter* said, this is a reason for being " filled with joy, though now for a little while you may have to suffer various trials " (*1 Pt* 1:6).

On this feast of Divine Mercy, the most beautiful message comes from Thomas, the disciple who arrived late; He was the only one missing. But the Lord waited for Thomas. Mercy does not abandon those who stay behind. Now, while we are looking forward

---

[44] Extract from the *Homily, Second Sunday of Easter* (or *Feast of Divine Mercy*), Church of the Holy Spirit in Sassia, 19 April 2020.

to a slow and arduous recovery from the pandemic, there is a danger that we will forget those who are left behind. The risk is that we may then be struck by an even worse virus, that of *selfish indifference*. A virus spread by the thought that life is better if it is better for me, and that everything will be fine if it is fine for me. It begins there and ends up selecting one person over another, discarding the poor, and sacrificing those left behind on the altar of progress. The present pandemic, however, reminds us that there are no differences or borders between those who suffer. We are all frail, all equal, all precious. May we be profoundly shaken by what is happening all around us: the time has come to eliminate inequalities, to heal the injustice that is undermining the health of the entire human family! Let us learn from the early Christian community described in the *Acts of the Apostles*. It received mercy and lived with mercy: "All who believed were together and had all things in common; and they sold their possessions and goods and distributed them to all, as any had need" (*Acts* 2:44-45). This is not some ideology: it is Christianity.

In that community, after the resurrection of Jesus, only one was left behind and the others waited for Him. Today the opposite seems to be the case: a small part of the human family has moved ahead, while the majority has remained behind. Each of us could say: "These are complex problems, it is not my job to take care of the needy, others have to be concerned with it!". Saint Faustina, after meeting Jesus, wrote: "In a soul that is suffering we should see Jesus on the cross, not a parasite and a burden... [Lord] you give us the chance to practice deeds of mercy, and we practice making judgements" (*Diary*, 6 September 1937). Yet she herself complained one day to Jesus that, in being merciful, one is thought to be naive. She said, "Lord, they often abuse my goodness". And Jesus replied: "Never mind, don't let it bother you, just be merciful to everyone always" (*Diary*, 24 December 1937). To everyone: let us not think only of our interests, our vested interests. Let us welcome this time of trial as an opportunity to prepare for our collective future, a future for all without discarding anyone. Because without an all-embracing vision, there will be no future for anyone.

Today the simple and disarming love of Jesus revives the heart of His disciple. Like the apostle Thomas, let us accept mercy, the salvation of the world. And let us show mercy to those who are most vulnerable; for only in this way will we build a new world.

To the World of Street Newspapers

The[45] lives of millions of people, who are already facing numerous difficult challenges in our world and are oppressed by the pandemic, have changed and are being seriously tested. Those most vulnerable, the invisible, those without an abode run the risk of paying the highest price.

I would therefore like to acknowledge the world of street newspapers, and especially their vendors, who are largely homeless, terribly marginalized and unemployed: thousands of people across the world who live and have a job thanks to selling these extraordinary newspapers.

In Italy, I think of the beautiful experience of the Caritas project *Scarp de' tenis*, which allows more than 130 people facing difficulties to have an income; and through it, to access fundamental citizens' rights. And not only that. I also think of the experience of more than 100 street newspapers throughout the world, published in 35 countries and in 25 different languages, that provide employ-

---

[45] *Letter*, 21 April 2020.

ment and an income to 20,500 homeless people in the world. For many weeks now, street newspapers have not been sold and their vendors cannot work. I would like therefore to express my solidarity with journalists, volunteers, and people living thanks to these projects who are doing everything they can these days through many innovative ideas.

The pandemic has made your work difficult but I am sure that the great network of street newspapers will come back stronger than ever. Turning our gaze to the poorest these days can help us all realize how much is actually happening to us, and what our condition truly is. My message of encouragement and brotherly friendship goes out to you all. Thank you for the work you do, for the information you provide, and for the stories of hope that you tell.

Overcoming Global Challenges

Dear[46] Brothers and Sisters, Good Morning!

Today we celebrate the fiftieth Earth Day. This is an occasion for renewing our commitment to love and care for our common home and for the weaker members of our human family. As the tragic coronavirus pandemic has taught us, we can overcome global challenges only by showing solidarity with one another and embracing the most vulnerable in our midst. The Encyclical Letter *Laudato si'* deals precisely with this "Care for our Common Home". Today, let us reflect together on that responsibility which characterizes "our earthly sojourn".[47]

We are fashioned from the earth, and fruit of the earth sustains our life. But, as the book of Genesis reminds us, we are not simply "earthly"; we also bear within us the *breath of life* that comes from God (cf. *Gen* 2:4-7). Thus, we live in this common home as one human family in biodiversity with God's other crea-

---

[46] *Wednesday Audience Catechesis on the Occasion of the 50th Earth Day*, 22 April 2020.

[47] *Laudato si'*, 160.

tures. As *imago Dei*, we are called to have care and respect for all creatures, and to offer love and compassion to our brothers and sisters, especially the most vulnerable among us, in imitation of God's love for us, manifested in His Son Jesus.

Because of our selfishness we have failed in our responsibility to be guardians and stewards of the earth. "We need only take a frank look at the facts to see that our common home is falling into serious disrepair".[48] We have polluted and despoiled it, endangering our very lives. For this reason, various international and local movements have sprung up in order to appeal to our consciences. I deeply appreciate these initiatives; still it will be necessary for our children to take to the streets to teach us the obvious: we have no future if we destroy the very environment that sustains us.

We have failed to care for the earth, our garden-home; we have failed to care for our brothers and sisters. We have sinned against the earth, against our neighbors, and ultimately against the Creator, the benevolent Father who provides for everyone, and desires us to live in communion and flourish together.

---

[48] *Ibid.*, 61.

How can we restore a harmonious relationship with the earth and with the rest of humanity? We need a new way of looking at our common home. It is not a storehouse of resources for us to exploit. For us believers, the natural world is the "Gospel of Creation": it expresses God's creative power in fashioning human life and bringing the world and all it contains into existence, in order to sustain humanity. As the biblical account of creation concludes: "God saw all that He had made, and it was very good" (*Gen* 1:31).

In today's celebration of Earth Day, we are called to renew our sense of sacred respect for the earth, for it is not just our home but also God's home. This should make us all the more aware that *we stand on holy ground*!

Dear brothers and sisters, "let us awaken our God-given aesthetic and contemplative sense".[49] The prophetic gift of contemplation is something that we can learn especially from indigenous peoples. They teach us that we cannot heal the earth unless we love and respect it.

At the same time, we need an ecological conversion that can find expression in con-

---

[49] Post-Synodal Apostolic Exhortation, *Querida Amazonia*, 2 February 2020, 56.

crete actions. As a single and interdependent family, we require a common plan in order to avert the threats to our common home. "Interdependence obliges us to think of one world with a common plan".[50] We are aware of the importance of cooperation as an international community for the protection of our common home. I urge those in positions of leadership to guide the preparations for two important international Conferences: *COP15 on Biodiversity* in Kunming, China, and *COP26 on Climate Change* in Glasgow, United Kingdom.

I would like to support concerted action also on the national and local levels. It will help if people at all levels of society come together to create a popular movement "from below". The *Earth Day* we are celebrating today was itself born in precisely this way. We can each contribute in our own small way. "We need not think that these efforts are not going to change the world. They benefit society, often unbeknown to us, for they call forth a goodness which, albeit unseen, inevitably tends to spread".[51]

In this Easter season of renewal, let us pledge to love and esteem the beautiful gift

---

[50] *Laudato si'*, 164.
[51] *Ibid.*, 212.

of the *earth*, our common home, and to care for all members of our human family. As brothers and sisters, let us together implore our heavenly Father: "Send forth your Spirit, O Lord, and renew the face of the earth" (cf. *Ps* 104:30).

INDEX